Little Maximus Myers

Sherry Boas

Illustrated by
Jeff West

Little Maximus Myers

Sherry Boas

Illustrated by Jeff West

Cover and book design: Tau Publishing Design Department
Author Photo: Adam Beltran

For information regarding permission, write to:
Tau Publishing, LLC
Attention: Permissions Dept.
4727 North 12th Street
Phoenix, AZ 85014

ISBN 978-1-61956-205-9

First Edition November 2013
10 9 8 7 6 5 4 3 2 1

Published and printed in the United States of America
by Tau Publishing, LLC
For additional inspirational books visit us at TauPublishing.com

TauPublishing.com

Words of Inspiration

For Maria, Michael, Teresa and John,
who inspire me
with their deep capacity for faith, hope and love.

On the day Maximus Myers was born, he was the tiniest bundle in the nursery. As he grew, he remained the smallest of all his friends. He couldn't ride his younger sister's low-rider trike because his feet didn't reach the pedals. His mom had to dress him in toddler clothes, which sometimes had embroidery of phony-looking T-rexes or silly phrases like "little slugger." Sometimes Maximus wondered why God made him so small.

To make matters worse, he wasn't fond of food. He saw eating as a waste of time when he could be pillow fighting with his brothers and sisters or setting up spy headquarters in the backyard tree house.

But one morning, while his family was out to breakfast after Sunday Mass, Maximus ordered the Deluxe Grand Emperor's Special from the adult menu. His parents looked at each other with wide, questioning eyes. His brothers and sisters snickered. The waitress smiled and returned a while later with a tray full of food for the Myers family, placing before Maximus a tall stack of buttermilk pancakes, three scrambled eggs, four halves of buttered toast, four strips of bacon, four sausage links, a side of hash browns and a tall glass of milk. In a matter of minutes, there was nothing left but two small triangle shaped remnants of pancake and a curl of bacon too small to mention.

"I'm going to eat a lot of food from now on, so I can grow big and strong and carry the cross," Maximus told the waitress when she cleared his plate with a look of buoyant approval.

For as long as he could remember, Maximus wanted to be an altar server and carry the crucifix in the procession at Holy Mass. But it dawned on him, as the procession passed one day, that only the tallest altar servers ever carried the enormous cross.

Although Maximus kept his word to that waitress and did indeed continue to eat heartily, he still grew very slowly. When he was in third grade, he was even smaller than some of the kindergartners. The team captain always chose him last, and he had to ask his younger brother to reach the glasses in the cabinet for him. Grown-ups rarely included him in discussions about his two favorite topics—politics and religion.

But life became much sweeter on the day that one of the deepest longings of his heart was finally fulfilled. After months of training, he was inducted into the ranks of St. Stephen's altar servers. People loved to see Maximus serve because he was so reverent, and they felt called into profound prayer by his example. People new to the parish would ask, "Who is that altar server—the littlest one? He is an angel. His feet don't even touch the ground." Maximus had such short legs he had no choice but to let his feet dangle when all the altar servers sat down during the readings.

While the larger altar servers were always assigned to carry the cross, Maximus was asked to carry candles or hold the lavabo for Father to wash his hands before saying the prayers that turn the bread and wine into the Body and Blood of Jesus.

One Sunday, Maximus was allowed to hold the large red book of opening and closing prayers for Father Adrian to read, but the boy was so short, he had to prop it atop his own head for the priest to see with his failing eyesight.

Maximus knew how very important his work was to Jesus and to all the people who would be united with Him in Holy Communion. But he still had a pious desire. He desperately wanted to carry the cross. Despite Maximus' frequent pleading, Sister Teresa, who was in charge of the altar servers, was afraid the tiny boy might have some sort of accident with a crucifix so heavy.

One day, when Maximus arrived for the 9 a.m. Mass, Sister was waiting outside the church, looking worried. "Thank goodness you're here, Maximus," she said. "You're the only one. The other two children who were scheduled to serve with you today are ill."

"Then, I will have to carry the cross!" Maximus felt a bit guilty for his excitement considering his fellow altar servers were sick.

"I don't think so, Maximus," Sister said.

Maximus' heart sank.

"I can do it, Sister," Maximus insisted. "Please. *Please.*"

Sister agreed to let him try to lift the crucifix out of its stand, certain that would put an end to Maximus' pestering. But to Sister's surprise, Maximus did it— without difficulty.

"Please, Sister," Maximus implored. "Just give me a chance."

"OK," Sister relented, looking more troubled than Maximus had ever seen her.

Immediately, his heart began to beat a little harder and his breath quickened, even as he tried to convince himself there was nothing to fear. All he had to do was carry the cross from the back of the church to the sanctuary and place it in its stand near the altar. He said a silent prayer to his guardian angel to help him.

When the opening hymn started and Maximus began the procession, he understood why Sister Teresa was so worried. The cross grew heavier with each step he took. This was much harder than it looked. One of the servers, in particular, had always made it appear so effortless. Michael was like a Marine, tall and straight, arms stiffly holding the cross square in front of his face, steady and still, as if it weighed nothing. That's how Maximus wanted to carry the cross.

But Maximus had taken less than a dozen steps, and already his legs were shaking, and the cross was wobbling. He couldn't hoist the cross up as far as the other servers did, so he had to walk with his feet wide apart, so as not to trip on it. He began to feel deprived of breath and the wood felt as if it would slip through his sweaty palms. The weight of the crucifix threw him off balance, and he staggered to regain his posture. The thought of dropping the cross and taking the congregation's attention off of Jesus was unbearable.

Maximus never realized before how massive was this church and how far away the altar was. And then it occurred to him, as he was about halfway there, that the worst was yet to come. With each step, he was getting closer and closer to the three sanctuary steps, which he would have to climb to place the cross in the stand near the altar. Panic now overtook him and he felt his arms beginning to shake as he realized there was no way to turn back and no way to keep going. Standing still was also not an option as a deacon and a priest were following behind him on the way to the altar to celebrate the most important event on the planet.

It was then that Maximus saw, in the deepest part of his heart, Jesus carrying His cross through the streets of Jerusalem, along the Via Dolorosa, nearing the hill of Calvary. Maximus realized how much heavier Jesus' cross was than the one he was carrying, how much more Jesus' body ached because of the terrible things his torturers had done to Him, how much weaker Jesus was because He had already travelled such a long way with the massive beams of wood bearing down on him. He wondered what kept Jesus' feet moving all the way to that horrible place where He would suffer so cruelly and die on the cross.

And then it occurred to him. (Maybe his guardian angel whispered it into his heart.) There is only one thing that is stronger than all of that pain.

Maximus continued to make his feet move, one step at a time, to the sanctuary steps.

"Your love for me carried your cross, Jesus," Maximus whispered under his breath. "My love for you will carry mine."

Up one step. His feet made an awkward landing, and the cross tottered.

Up again. The cross swayed backward.

Up once more. Maximus over-corrected and the cross arced so far forward, he was certain it was going down. He spent his final ounce of strength to heave the cross upright. He made it! He was in the sanctuary!

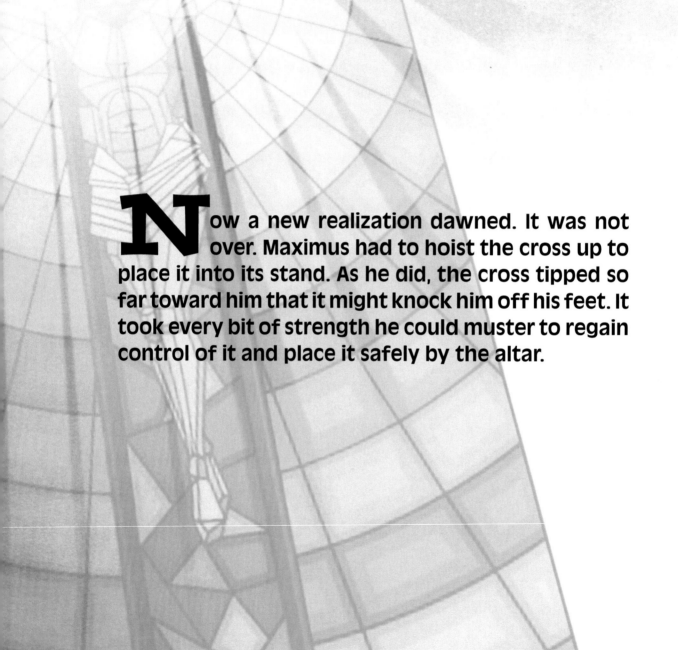

Now a new realization dawned. It was not over. Maximus had to hoist the cross up to place it into its stand. As he did, the cross tipped so far toward him that it might knock him off his feet. It took every bit of strength he could muster to regain control of it and place it safely by the altar.

Maximus' arms ached as he took his place near his chair, stood erect, hands together, fingers pointed toward heaven, waiting for the opening prayer.

For the first time ever in his life, Maximus was glad to be small and weak. He had felt the weight of the cross pressing down on him, and he had gotten a tiny taste of what his Savior suffered.

While the choir finished the last refrain, Maximus said a prayer of thanksgiving to his guardian angel and to the Blessed Trinity. To Jesus, for the suffering that bought us a place with Him in Heaven. To the Holy Spirit, for strengthening Maximus on his journey to the altar. And to the Father, for making him so small.

The
End

About the Author

Sherry Boas is author of the highly-acclaimed Lily Series, which began with *Until Lily* and has grown into an expanding collection of novels whose characters' lives are unpredictably transformed by a woman with Down syndrome. Her latest release is the fourth in the series: *The Things Lily Knew*.

Her first novel for youth, *Billowtail*, expected to be released in spring 2014, chronicles the adventures of a band of squirrels in search of a baby squirrel lost on the Way of St. James in Medieval Spain.

Boas is also author of *A Mother's Bouquet: Rosary Meditations for Moms* and the novel, *Wing Tip*, a unique tale of relentless love, celebrating the unfathomable mercy of God.

Little Maximus Myers is her first children's book.

She is owner of Caritas Press, publisher of a series of rosary meditations for moms, dads, children, teens, grandparents and altar servers.

Although she won numerous awards in her ten-year career as a journalist for a daily newspaper before her children were born, it was her vocation as a mother that would best prepare her for an author's career. For her, truth resounds and inspiration abounds in the struggles and triumphs of every-day family life.

Boas and her husband, Phil, are the joyful, special needs, adoptive parents of four warm-hearted and highly-adrenalized human beings, who make life rich beyond belief. They live in Arizona. You can find Boas' work at www.LilyTrilogy.com, CaritasPress.org, CatholicWord.com and in Catholic book stores nationwide. Also on Facebook: Sherry Boas Fan Page.